Todd Anderson about 12000 words
14017 Point Hills Cove
Draper, UT 84020
801-915-5443
Todd@PlatinumHR.com

HR CASE STUDIES:

WHAT TO DO WHEN YOU DON'T KNOW WHAT TO DO....

by

Todd Anderson, SPHR

Introduction

I wrote this at the prodding (read nagging) of a co-worker, Judy Tatton, who convinced me that the stories I shared with her in the office would make good reading for HR professionals and others. Hopefully the book can serve as a primer for budding HR professionals and a good learning tool for managers and leaders. I sincerely hope it will help you avoid some of the HR landmines that are out there. Lord knows that I've stepped on my share of them.

I hope you learn something new or that maybe you find yourself thinking around the corner for a better answer.....

What Makes a Good HR Professional?

For those of you who have the HR title on your business card, or who perform the HR function because it was handed to you along with 6 other jobs, you know how tricky it is to walk that fine line between wearing your corporate hat and being an advocate for the employees.

I have been in the Human Resources world for nearly 30 years now, working as an HR Manager in a small office of 30 people in Woodland Hills, California all the way up to a Regional Director of Human Resources for a Fortune 50 company in Salt Lake City, Utah with over 75,000 employees scattered around the world. I can tell you that walking that tight rope isn't always easy, but it is critical if you want to be a good HR Professional. In my opinion, there are two kinds of HR people. The first is the type that hides behind the curtain of Policies and Regulations. The type who never deviates from the policy and who opens the curtain once in a while to hand out a new policy. The second is the type who understands that policies are important to establish guidelines and set expectations, but someone who knows that there will always be an exception to the policy. The type who understands that there is a human behind every decision they make.

During my time in Salt Lake City, I was honored to be an HR consultant to the 2002 Salt Lake City Winter Olympics. How I got the assignment is a rather interesting story….. One day in late 2001, I was sitting in my office when I got a call from my former boss, Ed Eynon (a good friend and one of the best HR minds I have ever known). Ed had taken a position as the Vice President of Human Resources for the Salt Lake Organizing Committee which was hosting the 2002 Salt Lake City Winter Olympics. After a few minutes of catching up, he said that he had someone in his office who wanted to talk to me. Mitt Romney got on the line and said, "Todd, we need to find 27,000 volunteers for the 2002 Winter Olympics, how are you going to do that?" I responded with, "I have no idea, but we'll figure it out." For the next 6 months, my job was to design and implement a process whereby we could screen and enlist the help of over 27,000 volunteers.

The first and biggest hurdle we had to cross was finding people who could carve out 17 days from their work and family life to dedicate to the cause. We ended up screening over 100,000 applicants to fill the positions. What a terrific and rewarding experience! We still get feedback on how well the Olympics were run (due in no small part to Mr. Romney and his team) and how friendly and professionally the volunteers handled their assignments.

You might think that working at an Olympic venue would be glamorous and exciting and for some, it was. But for many of the volunteers, it was hard work and long hours for no pay. Some were ushers or helpers at the venues who got to see some of the events and rub shoulders with the athletes and visitors, but most of the volunteers were quietly doing their jobs behind the scenes, making sure the shuttles were running or that the parking lots were manned or the tickets were taken or the bathrooms were cleaned or the concession stands were running smoothly.

If you think about all the things that must happen in order to pull off an event of this size the logistics were daunting, but these wonderful volunteers came every day with a smile and a friendly greeting for everyone they met.

One of the smartest things we did was to tap into a very unique skill set that is found only in Utah: The thousands of missionaries from the LDS Church who call Utah home!

You are probably aware that Utah is the headquarters for the Church of Jesus Christ of Latter Day Saints (the Mormons). The Church has over 60,000 young men and women who serve as missionaries for the church. These dedicated young people voluntarily leave their homes for 2 years (1 ½ years for the women) to share their message with people all over the world. After serving their missions, many return home to Utah to continue their education or careers. Very early in the recruiting process, we contacted the Church leaders and asked for their help in getting the word out to this army of young men and women, many of whom had lived in foreign countries and spoke dozens of different languages.

Imagine their surprise and delight when a foreign visitor would show up at an event and have 15-20 young men and women standing in front of the venues with placards around their necks saying "We speak your language" in Italian, French, Portuguese, Tagalog, Mandarin, Russian, Italian, etc. The positive response we received from the visitors was overwhelming. They were so appreciative that someone spoke their language and could direct them or answer questions in their native tongue. Many of the volunteers even offered to drive their new friends around the city or meet them in the mornings to start their day. This was by far the smartest thing we did!

Fast forward to 2016. Today, I get to wear the HR consultant hat and I currently support over 1500 business clients in the western U.S.

I believe that one of the primary function of the HR professional is to keep the company out of legal hot water. How do we do that? To the degree possible, we become familiar with the various Federal, State and even City laws and regulations which govern the relationship between employer and employee and we try to communicate this to the members of Senior Management.

We should work closely with our operations partners to ensure that HR activities are within budget and, whenever possible, demonstrate value to the organization.

One of the most challenging and frustrating aspects of our job is to advise, consult and educate those in charge about the laws, regulations or policies knowing that we may not have the final say. We have to step back and let the President or the CEO or the Owner make the decision. There have been those few instances, where I have put my foot down and said, "we simply cannot do this" because of the extreme risk of a law suit, but for the most part, our job is to gain the respect of our business partners, educate them and hope they do the right thing.

Another key aspect of being an HR Professional is time management. One of the biggest challenges faced by HR professionals is that of managing your time effectively. In most professions, you can plan and schedule your day, set goals, and make widgets. Not so for the HR professional. I tracked my activities for an entire month early in my career and came to a startling conclusion. About 75% of my day was spent dealing with unexpected events! Even the 25% of my day that was my own was constantly interrupted by the emergencies. Here's a word of advice. When you plan your day, plan to be interrupted. Don't get frustrated when you can't accomplish all of your goals in a given day or week, because the bulk of your time as an HR Professional will be to put out fires.

Probably the most important part of HR is the idea that there are "humans" in the Human Resources equation. Behind every paycheck is a person. Someone who may have a family, someone who has a mortgage or rent to pay, someone who has to buy groceries, someone with a car payment, someone who may have something unpleasant going on at home....., you get the picture.

Part of this important "human" aspect of our jobs is to also remember that there are always two sides to every story. If a Supervisor or Manager storms into your office demanding that Sally be fired, remember something! The person telling you the story may have an ulterior motive and is probably tilting the story in his/her favor. Even when there seems little chance of a plausible explanation for the employee's behavior, everyone deserves his/her day in court and you may be surprised when you hear the other side of the story. I know I have been.

I firmly believe that a good HR professional should also be an advocate for the employees. To give voice to those who may not know how to voice their opinions. Again, this is a tricky proposition.

Do we recommend a raise for someone who is sitting in our office in tears because he/she can't pay their rent or make the car payment? Although we can sympathize with the employee, raises should be based on merit and performance, not on who can tell the saddest story.

Do we make exceptions for the employee who is constantly late because they have young kids at home or for the employee who is late because his car is old and always in the shop? The answer is…. It depends. I know, I know, I hate that answer too, but here are some things to consider:

- Is the behavior following a pattern or is it truly rare? Everyone understands that when someone is late or absent, it places a burden on everyone else to pick up the slack, but if the shoe were on the other foot and it was your car in the shop, wouldn't you want some leniency? There will always be things that happen which are beyond our control. Traffic, car troubles, kids are sick, I'm sick, bad weather, etc. Most companies have some kind of attendance policy that allows for a certain latitude when it comes to unexpected events, but if the behavior seems to be following a pattern or is excessive, we have a responsibility to the organization to enforce the policies and make sure that the company can make widgets.

- For you leaders out there, here's something else to consider. If you are seeing tardiness or absenteeism or laziness or behavior problems in an employee, guess who else is seeing it? Yup, everyone else in the office and they are looking to you to "fix" it. The longer the bad behavior is allowed to continue, the more respect and credibility Senior Management loses! And even though it feels like you are doing the kind thing by allowing certain employees more flexibility, being too tolerant may come back to bite you. If we have been overly indulgent to one person's plight and allowed them more time off than anyone else, longer lunches, extended leave, etc. and then we issue a verbal or written warning to someone else for the same infraction, their understandable reaction might be, "wait a minute, why am I being written up when Sally has been coming in late every day this week?" "Is it because of my age, race, religion, disability, …." You see where this could go sideways in a hurry. It's a fine line, but doing the right thing for the company might be doing the hard thing.

One last thought before we jump into the case studies. Have the courage to do the right thing! It's not easy and does take courage, but I think we all have a responsibility to stand up sometimes and tell the Emperor that he has no clothes on.

Several years ago, one of my co-workers didn't show up for work one day and didn't call her supervisor to tell her she wouldn't be that day. I had known this person for years and never known her to be irresponsible, so this was definitely out of character. The next day, she didn't show up for work and again and didn't call. Our company had a policy stating that 2 No-Call/No-Show events would be considered a voluntary resignation and we would terminate the employment relationship. We also had a policy stating that we would not pay out any unused vacation time unless the employee had given us two-weeks' notice (this happened to be in Utah, which allows employers to govern vacation/PTO accrual and payout), so we sent her final paycheck to the last known address ....minus her unused vacation time. The following week, I got a call from this friend and she told me that she had been in an abusive relationship and that her husband had beat her up the week before, so she had packed a bag, put her kids in the car and drove to her sister's home in California. She asked me if there was any way the company could pay out her unused vacation time to help her with groceries and other necessities.

I could have quoted her chapter and verse of the policy but, it wasn't the right thing to do! Did I make an exception to our policy? You bet I did! Would I do it again? In a heartbeat!

So, what are the risks of making exceptions to your company policy? What are the risks of setting a "precedent"? Well, they aren't as scary as they may seem. In my opinion, policies are designed to address about 95% of the situations you will face in your HR careers, but there will ALWAYS be situations that fall outside the scope of the policy and, as good HR professionals, we must have the courage to make exceptions if the situation warrants. Did I set a precedent with this employee? Yes! But setting a precedent simply means that if another situation pops up with the same set of circumstances, you would make the same exception! That's the right thing to do and the right way to manage your policies and procedures. The tricky part is remembering the circumstances under which you made the exception, so I highly recommend that you jot down some notes describing the situation and the reasons you made the decisions you did. Sometimes exceptions are warranted, but it takes courage to stand up and buck the system. Too often I hear things like, "we've never done that before", or "we've always done it that way". Just because a company has "never" done it or "always" done something a certain way doesn't make it right. Have the courage to do the "right" thing even if it means standing up to your boss and making your case.

Another example is when I was traveling from Salt Lake City to a small town in Colorado called Alamosa to conduct a workshop for some clients the following morning. My Delta flight to Denver was having mechanical problems and kept getting delayed which put me at risk of missing my connecting flight to Alamosa. I waited as long as I could, but eventually I had to run to the Southwest counter to see if they had a flight I could catch. Luckily, they did and I arrived in Denver with about 45 minutes to spare. If you have ever flown into the Denver airport, you know that is a very large, very sprawling airport and it took me nearly 30 minutes to make it to my connecting gate in the commuter annex of the airport. Great West Airlines has daily flights from Denver into Alamosa, so I raced up the counter only to see "Flight Cancelled" on the marquee. I tracked down one of the counter personnel and asked if there were any other flights going to Alamosa that night. She said that there was another flight leaving at 11:15 that night! It was about 5:00 p.m. and I have travelled enough to know that sometimes you have to give in to the travel gods and take your medicine, so I opened my Dean Koontz book and began to pass the time. There happened to be two others who were bumped from our original flight, an elderly woman who was easily in her 80's and her younger travelling companion. The sweet elderly woman struggled to walk and used a walker to get around. They too, sat down and began calling friends or family on the receiving end to let them know the flight had been canceled and that they would be on a different flight that wouldn't be arriving until after midnight. After about an hour, the travelling companion walked over to the ticket counter and asked the young lady working there if the airline would be issuing meal vouchers so the passengers could get something to eat in the airport. The young lady behind the counter had one of those faces that looked like she had been sucking on a lemon and had the disposition of the Soup Nazi from the old Seinfeld TV show. She told the travelling companion in no uncertain terms that there would be no meal voucher. The plucky companion asked to speak with a supervisor and was rewarded for her efforts. We all got a $5.00 meal voucher at McDonalds from the ticket Nazi. Here's where it got interesting. The McDonalds was a good 200 yards back into the main terminal, and there happened to be 3 or 4 wheelchairs lined up against the wall near the ticket counter. Without even thinking, the companion walked over and was about to take one of the chairs to push her friend to McDonalds so she could get a Big Mac. Guess who threw up all over that plan? You guessed it! Our friend the ticket Nazi. "You can't take one of those, that's against company policy!" she said. I was watching this whole scene unfold and thought to myself, "Really?" "Are you worried that the companion is going to steal your wheelchair?" "Are you worried that she is going to race down the hall and tip her elderly friend over?" Come on! Let's use some common sense here! Was it against company policy? Probably, but you know what? It's a stupid policy and it ought to be changed! The ticket Nazi made the companion put the chair back and called for someone to come and operate the "dangerous" wheelchair. 20 minutes later, a young man came and very kindly helped the elderly woman into the chair and did his job, but it was still 20 minutes of wasted time. If it were me, I would have let the companion "borrow" one of my wheelchairs so she could take her friend to get something to eat. If I got called on the carpet in front of my boss, I would have said, "yup, I let someone wheel her elderly friend to McDonalds and the policy is stupid and we need some latitude." Does that take courage? Maybe, but common sense seems to be waning in our society lately and it's time that those of us who have a fair dose, stand up and share a little with those who don't have the good sense God gave a soda cracker.

HR Case Studies……………..Thinking Around Corners

Before we begin dissecting some of these Case Studies, let's talk about some of the things to consider when dealing with Employee Relations issues. There are several questions I ask myself as I approach a new case. Sometimes I don't ask all of them, but I will certainly ask some of them. Here is my road map for investigating a sticky HR case:

1. Which law, regulation or policy is in play?
2. Who is or who could be the injured party?
3. What does the injured party want done?
4. What is the employer's responsibility?
5. What is the employee's responsibility?
6. What is the "right" thing to do?
7. Does the punishment fit the crime?

As we go through these case studies, I will try and walk you through the steps and how some or all of these questions helped me come to my decision. OK, let's get started. The first case, I call The Bathroom Photo Shoot.

The Bathroom Photo Shoot....

Here is the background:

A client of mine in a small, rural community of Utah happens to be a very large trucking firm. They have hundreds of trucks and drivers all over the United States. One day, a woman who works in the corporate office, left her desk to use the restroom. While in the restroom, she used the camera on her cell phone to take a picture of herself in a compromising position. This woman happened to be married, but she also had a boyfriend, which is neither here nor there, but it adds some complexity to our story. The woman sent the image to her boyfriend. It is important to point out that the boyfriend did not work for the company but he must have been dropped on his head as a child, because he decided to forward the image to one of his buddies, who did work for the company. As you can imagine, before the close of business, every trucker in the company had a picture of this woman on his phone,…….. including the woman's supervisor!! When the supervisor saw the image, he called the young lady into his office and asked, "What were you thinking?" Now, listen carefully to her response…..She asked, "Am I going to lose my job over this?" "I need the benefits for my family." "I can't believe that my co-workers would do this to me."

The senior management team convened an emergency meeting later that night to decide the fate of the employee. Their HR Director called me at 10:30 that evening, gave me the background information, put me on the speaker phone and asked what they should do. I asked, "What do you want to do?" He replied that they wanted to fire the woman, citing poor judgment, unprofessional behavior, etc. Here is where I started asking some of my roadmap questions.

Which laws apply?

Title VII defines Hostile Work Environment Sexual Harassment as,

"Unwelcome comments or conduct of a sexual nature that has the purpose or effect of unreasonably interfering with an individual's work performance or creating an intimidating, hostile, or offensive work environment."

Who is the injured party?

Was the female employee harassing her co-workers? No. She sent the image to a non-employee. Was her behavior a monumental example of poor judgment? A resounding yes! But which rule did she break? She was in the bathroom on a break, she used her own phone, and she sent the text to her boyfriend, not a co-worker. I submitted to the group, that as ironic as it may sound, she was the one being harassed! Remember, one of the definitions of Hostile Work Environment Sexual Harassment is when an employee is:

"telling lies or *spreading rumors of a sexual nature about a co-worker."*

Are her co-workers sending a sexually charged picture of one of their co-workers back and forth to each other and most assuredly calling each other to talk about the picture? YES.

If we fire her, she could not only sue the company for Hostile Work Environment Sexual Harassment, but for Retaliation as well!

Has she lodged a complaint? YES. Think about her comment to her Supervisor. "I can't believe my co-workers would do that to me". Even though it may not be in writing, I would say that she has put the company on notice that her co-workers are creating a hostile work environment.

Consider the definition of Retaliation:

> *Retaliation includes any adverse action taken against an employee for filing a complaint or supporting another employee's complaint under a variety of laws. The most common type of retaliation claim involves an employee who alleges that she was first harassed or discriminated against and later punished for making a complaint to her employer or a relevant federal agency.*

If the company fires this employee after she has lodged a complaint? Would she have legal grounds to sue the company for Retaliation? I have no doubt.

For years, race discrimination charges were the most common complaint against employers, but that has changed. The new #1 lawsuit according to the U.S. Equal Opportunity Commission, is Retaliation! In 2010, Retaliation cases totaled 36,258 and cost companies $404 million! This is the highest annual total ever that the EEOC has charged private sector employers. Not only that, but each lawsuit cost the employer over $100,000 to fight in court, regardless of the outcome!

Here's another point to consider! What about the Innocent Bystander Principle? The Innocent Bystander Principle states that:

> *"Employees have the right to come to work and do their jobs without being offended or made to feel uncomfortable by offensive comments, images or behavior they might see or hear even if the comments or actions are not directed at them."*

What if one of the truckers didn't want to see the image on his/her phone? Would this employee have grounds to file a complaint as an "innocent bystander"? Again, I think the answer is yes!

What does the injured party want done?

In this case, the woman just wanted to keep her job and for the behavior to stop. She didn't want anyone to lose their job.

Note: Just because the injured party wants something to happen, doesn't mean that the company must oblige. The injured party's request can certainly be taken into consideration in the decision-making process, but it shouldn't be only factor. Someone may want a co-worker fired for telling an off colored joke or story, for example, but is termination the correct and fair punishment for the crime? Maybe not.

What is the employer's responsibility?

Once I pointed out the finer points of my argument, the President said, "So, what should we do?" My suggestion was that he draft a very stern memo to everyone in the company (the woman included) generally rehearsing the company policy on Sexual Harassment and that if the company learned that this kind of behavior was happening, it would take appropriate steps to make it stop. He agreed and the woman is still employed, but with a new appreciation for the dangers of pushing the "send" button on her cell phone.

Hey Buddy, Can You Help Me Out?

Here's the background:

One of my clients in Salt Lake City, Utah had a drug policy which allowed them to randomly test its employees once per month. Their protocol was that, once notified, the employee had two hours to report to the clinic to provide a urine sample. On the appointed day, one of the employees got tapped on the shoulder and was told to report to the clinic. We found out later that this employee had partied the night before and smoked marijuana, so he knew his test would come back positive for illegal drugs! What to do?? He came up with a brilliant plan! On his way to the clinic, he stopped at the local drug store and purchased a package of balloons and proceeded to drive to a friend's house. Yes, you can see where this is going! He asked his buddy to urinate in the balloon so the employee could pass the drug test. The friend agreed and the employee carried the urine-filled balloon to the drug testing facility and provided his sample. All's well that ends well, right? Well, not so fast. The test results came back positive…….. for cocaine!! Yup, the buddy didn't bother to tell the employee that he had used cocaine earlier…. Some friend!! You may be wondering how the HR Manager knew all the details? When the HR Manager confronted the employee, his response was….you guessed it! "It's not mine!" And he proceeded to spill the beans on his buddy. Obviously, to no avail!

Which laws apply?

The State of Utah allows employers to randomly test its employees, so that's legal. The company had a policy that notifies employees of the random tests (the employee had signed on the dotted line), so the employer had the right to conduct the test and take whatever actions it deemed appropriate. The lesson for HR Professionals from our story is two-fold:

1) It is my experience that drug users are very savvy when it comes to cheating the system. There are all kinds of "kits" one can buy to cheat, from synthetic urine kits, to "flush" kits, etc. My advice when administering any kind of drug/alcohol test, is that you give the participant a minimal amount of time to provide a urine sample. I would say no more than 30 minutes. Less, if possible.

2) The other action item from out story would be for the employer to notify the testing facility that their process is flawed. There should have been checks in place to catch someone emptying a balloon into a sample container.

Who is the injured party?

In this case, the employer is the injured party. It established policies and procedures to prevent its employees from being under the influence of drugs or alcohol at work. The employee may have posed a safety risk to himself or others or his performance may have suffered because of his impairment.

What is the employer's responsibility?

The employer has a responsibility to provide a safe and productive work environment for all of its employees. If someone is impaired and potentially putting him/herself or others at risk, the employer has an obligation to remove the risk. The employer also has a responsibility to be profitable. If the impaired employee is not producing or is producing an inferior product, the company suffers. Some companies have also taken the position that they will notify authorities if they discover illegal drugs in the test. All of these things must be considered when administering a drug/alcohol policy.

Here are some interesting things to consider when it comes to drug/alcohol testing. 73% of all current drug users aged 18 and older (8.3 million adults) were employed in 1997. This includes 6.7 million full-time workers and 1.6 million part-time workers.[1] The DOL has not published an updated number as of this date, but one can assume that the number is the same or higher today. If your company is not doing some sort of drug testing, you must ask yourself if some of these drug users are working for you? They are working somewhere!

According to USAToday, the price of one pure gram of cocaine has increased by 47% since 2006, selling for $137 for one gram. A cocaine addict can easily spend $100 per day on cocaine. Methamphetamine is proving to be one of the most expensive drugs on the street. The going rate for one pure gram of Meth is around $245, which is a dramatic leap from $133 in 2006. Meth users may spend more than $1,000 per week. Addicts are getting the money somewhere. Are they stealing from you? Are they stealing from customers? Are they stealing from their co-workers? The National Institutes of Health recently reported that alcohol and drug abuse cost the economy $246 billion in 1992, the most recent year for which economic data are available.[6] If your company doesn't have a drug testing policy, I would highly recommend that you consider one.

Several years ago, I started working for a company that did not have a drug policy. It was a call-center business with hundreds of Customer Service Representatives on the phones 24/7. It was a disaster. We had undercover narcotics police officers working for us. They were trying to catch the dealers who were out on our production floor. We would find used syringes and other drug paraphernalia in the restrooms weekly.

Remember that the drug community is fairly tight knit and if one of the drug users works for your company and you don't drug test, guess who they will be calling when there is a job opening? You can hear the conversation now, "Hey, come to work here. They don't drug test." Is that a risk your company is willing to take? I hope not. Drug and alcohol addiction are insidious and destructive. These people need help, but the workplace is not a rehab center. We have widgets to make!

Does the punishment fit the crime?

This is a tough question. Do you give the employee time off to get help? Do you fire them outright? Only you can decide, but here are some thoughts: If you decide to allow the addict to seek treatment, you must insist that they provide you with a certificate of completion from their health care professional and then I would let the returning employee know that, as a condition of their continued employment, he/she will be randomly tested for the next several months. The test will be completely at the employer's discretion.

If you decide to terminate the employment relationship, you are well within your legal right to do so. Recently Colorado and Oregon have passed laws legalizing the recreational use of marijuana, Marijuana is still listed as a Schedule 1 Controlled Substance under the Federal Controlled Substances Act and the employer has the right to implement and enforce a zero tolerance drug policy to include marijuana even in those States. Employees may argue that Marijuana is legal in you State, so you shouldn't penalize them for being under the influence. My counter argument to that is, "alcohol is also a legal substance, but that doesn't mean I am going to let you come to work impaired."

I Hope I'm Not Interrupting…..

Here's the background:

A client called one morning and left a message asking me to call her back. I didn't know this at the time, but one of the client's male employees (let's call him Tom to keep the players straight) stepped into the restroom and heard someone masturbating (let's call this employee Bill) in the stall next to his. It made him feel uncomfortable, so he reported the incident to his Supervisor. The Supervisor reported the incident to the HR Manager and the Manager called me and left a message for me to call her back.

This is scene I of our little production. Scene II unfolded in the couple of hours it took me to call her back.

The curtain opens on Scene II when the Supervisor tells the story to several of his co-workers and as you can imagine, the story spread like wildfire through the entire facility.

What laws apply?

<u>Hostile Work Environment Sexual Harassment?</u> I think so. Title VII defines <u>Hostile Work Environment Sexual Harassment</u> as,

"Unwelcome comments or conduct of a sexual nature that has the purpose or effect of unreasonably interfering with an individual's work performance or creating an intimidating, hostile, or offensive work environment."

I think the Innocent Bystander Principle would apply here as well. The behavior was probably not intended for Tom to hear, but he overheard Bill's behavior and it made him feel uncomfortable.

Who is the injured party?

This is where it gets interesting! In Scene I, Tom is the injured party. He was offended by behavior of a co-worker so he reported the incident to his Supervisor. Had Scene II not occurred, this would have been relatively easy to resolve. HR would have taken Tom's statement, called Bill into the office to hear his side of the story and ascertain whether the story was true and if so, whether Bill had any plausible reason for his behavior. I know! Unlikely, but remember everyone deserves his/her day in court and as unlikely as it may seem, there could be a legitimate reason for the behavior. I thought of one: Let's say that Bill is married and he and his wife are trying to get pregnant. They aren't having any luck, so they go to an Urologist, who diagnoses Bill with a low sperm count and prescribes hormone therapy to increase Bill's sperm count. The doctor instructs Bill to collect samples at different times during the day to see if the medication is having any effect. Is it possible? Yes. Is it probable? I'll let you decide. At any rate, HR would gather the facts and make a determination. If Bill was following his doctor's orders, maybe we could find him a more private place. If Bill were simply pleasuring himself, we would let him know that work is not the appropriate place for this and let him know that it can't happen again.

Scene II complicates things exponentially! Now who is the injured party? You guessed it! Bill! Are his co-workers spreading stories of a sexual nature about him? Yes. So now what do we do? My recommendation was to call Bill into the office and have the Scene I discussion with him about his behavior in the bathroom and then launch into the second discussion to help him understand what the company was doing to resolve the mess from Scene II. After Bill leaves the office, I would immediately call the Supervisor into the office and hear his side of the story. At this point, I can't imagine any plausible explanation for this behavior, but I would be willing to listen. Failing any explanation that made sense, the Supervisor would receive a written warning for gross violation of sensitive information and creating a Hostile Work Environment for Bill. If this was a pattern of behavior for the Supervisor, this may have been the straw that broke the camel's back and he would be out of a job. I would then try and learn to whom the Supervisor had talked and try to get the toothpaste back in the tube. I would talk with each employee who had knowledge of the event and make it very clear to them that they are not to share the story with anyone at work and that if we hear a peep from them, there will be serious consequences.

Who could be the injured party?

In this case, I don't know if Bill knew that the story was floating around the shop, but he certainly was the injured party and I think it is better to bring the matter to his attention proactively rather than waiting for him to find out through the grapevine and then come storming back into the office demanding satisfaction.

My Kingdom for a Vegan!!

One of my favorite clients operates an animal shelter in a small town in Southern Utah. They are the largest employer in the area with over 400 wonderful people who take care of abandoned and abused animals. They have over 3700 acres which houses reserves for horses, dogs, cats, rabbits, pigs, etc. As you might imagine, the people who work for this company are kind, dedicated, caring individuals. The owner happens to be vegan and when the CEO retired, he went to the HR Manager and instructed her to look for a replacement, but the new CEO must be vegan also!

The HR Manager called and asked if she could do that.

What laws apply?

I searched and searched but couldn't find any law that protected Carnivores, so I had to admit that there were no laws that protected someone who had a big juicy steak now and again. I did have a reality check discussion with her however. First, she was trying to fill a CEO position for a large organization. That pool is pretty shallow to begin with. Next you are looking for someone who lives in or would be willing to relocate to a small town in Southern Utah. The pool just got shallower. Lastly you want to find someone with these qualifications and you want them to be Vegan. Are you sure that owner won't bend a little on this requirement? As an at-will employer, they can hire whoever they want to, so I wished them my best and promptly went to In-N-Out and ordered a Double/Double animal style!

Body Parts in the Parking Lot

Here's the background:

One day, a client called and said that one of her employees had just left her office and had complained about something she had seen in the parking lot that offended her. One of the other employees who owned a pickup truck had some of those rubber testicles hanging from his trailer hitch. The woman saw the testicles and was offended.

Which Laws apply:

As good HR folks, we want to be open minded and explore all sides of the situation, so I would first look at whether we have a Hostile Work Environment Sexual Harassment case here. Remember, Hostile Work Environment is defined as:

> *"Unwelcome comments or conduct of a sexual nature that has the purpose or effect of unreasonably interfering with an individual's work performance or creating an intimidating, hostile, or offensive work environment."*

The first thing I would decide is whether the parking lot is part of the work environment? In this case it was space leased by the company. If someone were physically harassing an employee in the parking lot, would I step in and try to stop it. Absolutely. So, is this any different? I think the conclusion I would have to come to is that the parking lot is part of the work environment and a place over which I need to exercise some control.

Next I would try and determine whether the behavior *"has the purpose or effect of unreasonably interfering with an individual's work performance or creating an intimidating, hostile, or offensive work environment."*

I doubt that the owner of the truck is intentionally trying to interfere with anyone's work performance, but is the behavior creating an offensive work environment? Obviously, someone thinks so!

Here are some of the thoughts that went through my head:

After the famous Clarence Thomas sexual harassment trial in 1991, there was such an influx of Sexual Harassments and complaints that it was bogging down the system. Some of the allegations were legitimate and needed to be addressed, others were frivolous and needed to go away, but how do we know which is which? Sandra Day O'Conner, a Supreme Court Justice at the time, wrote a legal opinion which stated that when in doubt, we should rely on the "Reasonable Prudent Person Test". The reasonable test would ask what a reasonable person OF THE SAME SEX as the injured party would say about the behavior. Notice that Justice O'Conner was careful to specify someone of the same sex as the offended party, because, let's face it, men and women view the world very differently. So, I asked the HR Manager, who happened to be a woman and who seemed reasonably prudent, how she perceived the truck ornament? She said that it didn't bother her, so we put a mark on the side of the ledger that says, "maybe this isn't a big deal".

Another consideration would be to consider the culture or the environment in which you find yourself. Had this happened at a hunting lodge in Casper, Wyoming where the testicles would probably be handed out to employees as standard issue, this client operated a business in the downtown area of Salt Lake City, so the culture question might say that propriety and decorum could be part of the equation.

The HR Manager and I talked about this for quite a while and concluded that even though an employee had lodged a complaint, it didn't rise to the level of any "official" action. I suggested that she could call the truck owner in and explain the situation and see if he would be willing to leave his testicles home when coming to work. Or maybe he could park on the street that wasn't controlled by the company. But, if he refused, did this rise to the level of an official reprimand? I didn't think so and the female HR Manager agreed.

Who is the injured party?

In this case, the injured party is the woman who lodged the original complaint. Do we have an obligation to hear the complaint and take "appropriate" action? Absolutely. In this case, the HR Manager and I agreed that no official action needed to be taken. She was going to have a reasonable conversation with the truck owner, but it may not change anything. This may just be a case where someone is overly sensitive to certain behavior at work and the injured party may just have to look away when passing by the truck. We are never going to make everybody happy. As badly as we would like to, it just isn't possible. Our job is to use common sense and try to keep the peace as best we can.

While we're on the subject of parking lots, let's explore some other scenarios. What if someone comes to work with a Swastika bumper sticker on the back of their vehicle? What if a bumper sticker is obscene or vulgar or religiously offensive? What if someone is smoking in the parking lot? What if someone has a gun in a vehicle in the parking lot? Interesting questions. Let's explore them.

For offensive, vulgar or obscene images or behavior, the Reasonable Prudent Person Test is the default. Oftentimes HR can act as the reasonable prudent person and can make a decision on the fly, but when in doubt, it never hurts to bring someone else in the story and get his/her opinion and then take appropriate action

Smoking is interesting. Most companies have policies that restrict smoking to only certain areas of the property that have been designated as smoking areas. If the parking lot is not a designated smoking area and your company leases the parking space, you have the right to counsel the smoker on their behavior. Here is something else to consider when it comes to smoking in the parking lot. Did you know that the liquid form of gasoline is not the most combustible part of the fuel mixture? It's actually the fumes! Do gas stations allow patrons to smoke while filling their car with gas? Of course not! The parking lot could also be a dangerous place to smoke?

A gun in vehicles is also an interesting discussion. Several states have adopted "workplace protection" gun statutes which allow concealed handgun licensees to keep a handgun in their personal vehicle on their employer's parking lot. The statutory language varies greatly, but the laws essentially "prohibit both public and private employers from restricting their employees' possession of firearms." States that have enacted workplace protection laws include Maine, Florida, Georgia, Kentucky, Mississippi, Utah, Minnesota, Kansas, North Dakota, Oklahoma, Texas, Indiana, Idaho, Arizona, Louisiana. HR professionals should research their State's laws regarding "workplace protection laws".

I've Hired a Witch!

Here's the background:

A client of mine has several offices in Idaho. He hired a young lady to work for him in one of the offices and after a few weeks somehow discovered that she was a member of the local Wicca chapter. Wicca is the religion practiced by witches. No, they don't fly around on brooms or wear a big, black hat. They worship nature and don't believe in hurting anything, even insects. Wiccans heal illnesses with herbs. My client called me and told me that he was worried that in small Idaho towns, some people may not understand the religion and choose not to frequent his business. He wanted to know if he could fire her……

Which laws apply?

This one is pretty easy. Title VII specifically identifies religion as a protected class. The EEOC has taken it a step further and stated that an employer must also grant reasonable accommodations for an employee's religion as long as it doesn't pose a hardship to the organization.

Let's talk about this for a minute. Before we can accommodate someone's religion, we must first understand the definition of "religion". It's not as simple as it sounds. In fact, it gets rather complicated. Title VII protects religious beliefs, practices, and observances, including those that are traditionally theistic (believing in a god or gods) in nature as well as "moral or ethical beliefs as to what is right and wrong which are sincerely held with the strength of traditional religious views. This is where it gets tricky. Reasonable accommodations can take many forms depending on the circumstances, from allowing employees to wear certain clothing, to granting them time or days off for religious observances. The definition of "hardship" is a moving target and depends on many factors. The EEOC has said that a financial hardship is anything with more than a "de minimus" cost, yet they have failed to define "de minimus".

Some other things to consider might be the type of industry in which you operate. Your company may have a policy that says, "no hats" or that "hair for men must be kept short and well groomed" or "no beards". Let's say you hire a man who belongs to the Sikh faith and he asks you for an accommodation to grow a beard and wear a turban. It would be important to understand that the men who have been baptized or undergone their religion's initiation ceremonies in the Sikh religion don't cut their hair and they wear turbans. Baptized Sikh women wear a turban or a scarf. If you run a factory with lots of moving parts, loose fitting clothing, headgear, scarves or even beards may pose a safety hazard, remember….safety always trumps a request for a religious accommodation! The best way to head this off at the pass is to ensure that you have explained the nature of the job in the interview and explored whether the employee can perform the duties of the job. Will employees always disclose their religion or religious requests in a job interview? Probably not. In fact, even having a discussion about religion could get you in trouble. So, how do you handle requests for religious accommodations? First, consider every request that you receive and take it seriously. Look at all the angles.

There was a case of a Border Patrol agent in Arizona who had been working the weekend shift for years, but had recently converted to the Seventh Day Adventist faith, which recognizes its Sabbath from Sundown on Friday to sundown on Saturday. He asked his supervisor if he could have Saturdays off to attend his church and honor his religion. The supervisor made the mistake of pulling out the Agent's signed offer letter with the schedule clearly marked and telling the Agent to get back to work. The Agent sued and won for religious discrimination. The Supervisor's mistake wasn't necessarily denying the request, it was failing to go through a due diligence process to discover if the request was reasonable. Had the Supervisor attempted to accommodate the Agent by seeing if he could switch shifts with another Agent, or switch days off, he could have gone back the Agent and said, "I tried. These are the things that we looked at and we just couldn't find a way to accommodate your request. We need you to work your shift." Had the Supervisor done that, I seriously doubt that they would have lost the law suit. The mistake the Supervisor made was that he didn't even try.

Here's another example: In a previous life, I was a Regional HR Director for a very large Customer Care business. I had responsibility for 5 call centers with over 6000 employees. One of the centers was in Moore, Oklahoma, where had over 1000 employees working in the facility at any given time. We had hired several employees who belonged to the Muslim faith. As you may know, their religion encourages them to pray 5 times per day. Several of these employees approached their Supervisor and asked if the company would be willing to grant them an extra break during the day so they could offer their prayers.

Luckily, I had a wonderful HR Manager working for me by the name of Mike Dill. I'll have to tell you a couple of quick stories about Mike to give you some background on this great man. Mike was a retired Colonel from the U.S. Army. Mike still has the bulldog haircut and the sharp military posture and is a great American. Mike served in Viet Nam and his job was to parachute with his German Sheppard behind enemy lines and live for weeks at a time taking out command and control personnel. Needless to say, you didn't mess with Mike! Mike's daughter happened to be a cheerleader at the local high school during the time I knew Mike and one day Mike and his wife went to one of the high school football games to watch their daughter cheer. Before the game, the high school band started playing the National Anthem as the High School ROTC presented the colors. The audience stood and most of the audience removed their hats….. notice that I said most. There was a young man in front of Mike who hadn't removed his baseball cap, so Mike politely leaned over and asked the young man to remove his cap. Instead of complying, the young man made the mistake of showing Mike his middle finger…. Now, remember who we are dealing with here. This is a retired Army Colonel who had fought for his country and stood tall in hell on many occasions. Rather than making a scene, Mike reached over and gently removed the young man's hat for him. Well! The young man didn't like that one bit, so he ran off to tell daddy. A few minutes later, the father came marching up the bleachers and confronted Mike and said, "so, what's the big idea?". Mike looked the taller man in the eye and said, "sir, I've lost good friends and brothers who fought for what that song and that flag represents. I asked your son to remove his cap during the playing of the National Anthem and he flipped me off, so I removed his hat for him." You know what the father did? He took his son by the ear, said, "thank you" to Mike and marched his son behind the bleachers. Anyway, that's Mike. So, back to our story with our Muslim employees. Mike very patiently listened to their request and called me to get my thoughts. We all agreed that to give these few employees an extra 10-minute break during the day wasn't going to cause an undue hardship on the company, so we allowed them an extra break during their shift. Did this set a precedent? Yes. Would we grant someone else a similar accommodation if they came to us with similar reasonable religious request? Yes. Let's remember something here, though. This was an environment where we had hundreds of other employees to pick up the slack for these few who took an extra break. What if this was a manufacturing environment where your employees are working at an assembly line and widgets are coming at them? Now the request for an extra break might pose a hardship for the company. Breaks and lunches in this environment are usually scheduled to ensure coverage and maximum efficiency. One person not doing his job affects the rest of the line. The point I'm making here is that before you simply say "no" to a request, especially if it is a religious request, stop and consider whether the request is reasonable and whether the accommodation poses a hardship to the company. The EEOC has defined a hardship as a situation that "places an undue burden on the company………."

"The Feet Were Pointed the Wrong Way"

Here's the background:

One of the call-center facilities I oversaw was located in a town called Pharr, Texas. I had a terrific HR Manager named Frank Gomez who did a good job of herding the cats in his facility, but one day he called and said, "Todd we have a problem and I'm not quite sure how to handle it." When I asked what was going on, Frank told me that they had hired a young man several weeks before to work as a Customer Service Representative on the phones. Let's call our employee John for the sake of this discussion. John had made it through training and had been on the production floor for a couple of weeks, but this day John came to work dressed as a woman!

Which law applies?

Currently, there are no state laws in Texas that prohibit employment discrimination based on sexual orientation or gender identity, although five of Texas's six largest cities have local ordinances partially banning such discrimination in specific cases. Be sure to check your State law regarding Sexual Orientation, Gender Identity, Transgender, etc. The following website from the ACLU provides a map and some good information: http://www.aclu.org/maps/non-discrimination-laws-state-state-information-map.

With no law in place, we then looked at our company policy to see it would provide any direction. Some companies will have a Dress Code Policy that is gender specific and will outline acceptable dress for men and women. Our policy was generic and gender neutral, so that didn't help us.

As part of the discussion, I asked Frank if John had any problems with his attendance? Nope. Is he getting along with his co-workers? Yup. Is he doing a good job? Yup. Does he take direction from his Supervisor? Yup. So Frank and I concluded that, as long as he was doing his job and wasn't disrupting the workplace with his behavior, we should live and let live. I did suggest that we call John into the office just so we could understand where he was coming from and maybe be sensitive to what was going on in his life. Frank called John into the office and we learned that John was in the process of changing his identity from male to female. He told us that his Doctor was making him live the lifestyle of a woman for 1 year before the surgery to make sure John really wanted the operation. So, John was growing his hair, wearing make-up, wearing women's clothing, taking hormone pills which caused him to develop breasts, etc. We thanked John for being candid and told him we would do what we could to be supportive.

After about 2 months had gone by, Frank called me one day and said, "Todd, we have another issue with John!" I asked what had happened and Frank proceeded to tell me that he had a Sexual Harassment complaint sitting on his desk from a young lady. Before I tell you the rest of the story, you need to understand our environment. The building we occupied was a Walmart building we had purchased and converted into a call center. The offices were situated around the perimeter of the space with the bays of work stations in the large open area in the middle. The bathrooms were the original dormitory-style restrooms with multiple stalls for the women and multiple stalls and urinals for the men.

The sexual harassment complaint had been filed by a young lady who was in the women's restroom seated in one of the stalls. She heard someone enter the stall next to hers and begin to urinate, but….. she noticed that the feet were pointed the wrong way! She realized that there was a man in the stall next to her and it made her feel uncomfortable so she lodged a complaint.

We immediately applied the Reasonable Prudent Person test by presenting a "hypothetical" situation to several of our female co-workers and even though some didn't seem to mind, most of the women agreed that it would make them feel uncomfortable having a man in the women's restroom. So, we knew we had to do something.

We explored all of the options we could think of, but couldn't come up with one that was quick and simple. Remember, we didn't have a unisex/single-stall bathroom in the building. We only had the multiple stall versions. We thought about building out a unisex bathroom, but there was a cost and certainly a time element that didn't make this the quickest solution, although we kept it on the table as an option and put that on our list of maintenance projects for the future, but that didn't solve our immediate problem. We then thought "if he is living the lifestyle of a woman, we might ask him to be more discrete and sit down when he uses the restroom". The problem with that idea was that we already had one person who knew his true identity and she didn't want him the restroom. It was a safe bet that other women would feel the same way, so that wasn't the most elegant solution. Next, we explored the anatomical option. John's plumbing hadn't changed yet, so anatomically he was still a guy. We could require that John use the men's restroom but……. we were trying to be sensitive to John's situation and we also wanted to be sensitive to the rest of the workforce too. It didn't seem very sensitive to force John into the men's restroom, an environment where he didn't want to be. We also looked at it from a guy's perspective. Imagine that you are a male employee standing at the urinal, when in walks this person dressed as woman. I know as a guy that would make me uncomfortable! We even thought about renting one of those construction Porta-Potty units that we could place outside the building, but that just didn't seem right either. This was in Southern Texas….. in the summer……not a pleasant thought. We were stuck!! We didn't have a good solution!

Here's another tidbit of HR wisdom that I have acquired over the years. Sometimes it makes sense to bring the person in question into the discussion to see if they can help solve your problem. So that's what we did. Frank called John into the office and the three of us talked about the situation. First of all, John was mortified that he had not been more discreet and he felt horrible that he had made is female co-worker feel bad. We told John that we had run into a brick wall and that we couldn't think of a great solution for our predicament. John thought for a minute and finally said, "I have an idea. The company has a policy that prohibits employees from leaving the building during our paid breaks, but if you will make an exception for me, I will clock out on my breaks and go across the street to use the single stall bathroom in the convenience store." Frank and I both agreed that this would be a quick way to resolve the issue, so we thanked John for his input and made an exception to our policy. Did it make sense? I think so. Was it the right thing to do? Under the circumstances, it bought us some time until we could build out the single stall bathroom in our building.

Who is the injured party?

In this case, the woman who lodged the initial complaint is our injured party, so after we came to our solution, we communicated to the woman that John would not be allowed to use the women's bathroom. She didn't need to know the details, just that her complaint had been heard and resolved.

This is a good time to discuss how we treat those who lodge legitimate complaints. One of the steps I always follow is to ask the injured party what he/she wants to have happen. It doesn't mean that we always follow the suggestion, but we should always consider it.

Onion Boy

A client called one day and was telling me the story about one of their employees, let's call him Phil, who was constantly complaining about one thing or another. We all know the type. He was one of our "problem children" who never graduated from the Sandbox 101 class and was never happy. Anyway, the client was telling me that now Phil was complaining about his co-workers leaving half-eaten food in the waste baskets and that the smell of onions was bothering him. The client had tried to work with Phil over the years with his complaints that the warehouse was too hot, or it was too cold or it was Thursday and he wanted it to be Friday. You get my drift. When Phil started complaining about the food smell, some of his co-workers started calling him Onion Boy. Well, one day Onion Boy passed out at work and had to be rushed to the emergency room for a severe allergic reaction to ……….. you guessed it………..onions! Come to find out, there is a small number of people who are deathly allergic to onions and other plants classed as Alliums. Other members of that family include chives, leeks, shallots, scallions and garlic. Some of the symptoms include coughing or congestion, vomiting, fainting, a skin rash or hives and swelling of the face, tongue, windpipe or other part of the body. The swelling may even make breathing impossible or very difficult. In this case, it caused Phil's throat to constrict and make it very difficult for him to breathe.

What laws apply.

The Americans with Disabilities Act defines a disability as, *"a physical or mental impairment that substantially limits one or more major life activities, a record of such impairment, or regarded as having an impairment."*

Does Phil have a condition that substantially limits one or more of his life functions? How about breathing? I would say that would be important life function! So, what is an employer's responsibility when dealing with employees who have disabilities? Here are some key things to remember. The Americans with Disabilities Act only legally applies to those employers with 15 or more employees on the payroll. Why 15? I have no idea. If we are going to try and work with those who have disabilities, why draw the line at 15? I think "morally" we draw the line at 1 employee, but then I'm not a politician. I'm just an HR guy living in the real world. Anyway, if your company has 15 or more employees, you are now bound by the Americans with Disabilities Act which says that if someone comes to a member of management and begins to describe a condition that might be a disability, we are obligated to engage that employee in an interactive dialogue to discover whether the condition truly is a disability and what, if any, accommodations can we consider that will allow the employee to perform the essential duties of his/her job? There are a lot of moving parts in that last idea, so let's make sure we understand what they mean.

If an employee claims to have a disability, even though the employee doesn't use the word *disability* or invoke his/her right to protection under the ADA, we cannot ignore it or pretend we didn't hear it. We have to explore it! What does that mean? One thing we can do and I highly recommend, is that we get medical verification of the disability. Obviously if someone is in a wheelchair or is blind or is missing a limb, we don't need a Doctor to confirm the disability, but many of today's disabilities are not easily detectable. Below is a list of the various life activities that have been identified by various Federal agencies, including the EEOC and even the Supreme Court:

Caring for oneself

Performing manual tasks

Sitting

Walking

Learning

Hearing

Speaking

Breathing

Concentrating

Thinking

Interacting with others

Bending

Communicating

Working

Sitting

Standing

Lifting

Sleeping

Reaching

Seeing

Concentrating

Eating

Reading

2008 Amendment states that a major life activity also includes: "*operation of a major bodily function, including but not limited to, functions of the immune system, normal cell growth, digestive, bowel, bladder, neurological, brain, respiratory, circulatory, endocrine, and reproductive functions.*"

I don't know about you, but I see a couple of things on there that qualify me as disabled!!

As you can see, there is the possibility that many of your employees might have a reason to approach you and share with you some information that might be a disability.

So, now that we have determined that our employee has a disability, what do we do? The first thing is to ascertain whether the employee can perform the essential duties of his/her job with or without an accommodation. Enter the job description! Job descriptions are the foundation on which so many things happen in HR. Hopefully your job descriptions outline the various job functions of the position, but more importantly, it specifically describes the "essential duties". Unless we have identified these essential duties, a discussion around the ADA becomes very difficult. For example, if your company makes televisions and the company's quota each day is to ship 100 televisions out the door. One of your employees comes to you and says that his doctor has told him that he has arthritis in his elbows and back and the arthritis is limiting his ability to lift and bend so he can only move 90 televisions across his work station each day. If your job description has identified "moving 100 televisions across your work station" as an essential duty, we can have a meaningful conversation about reasonable accommodations. We might consider something like a Velcro back brace to support the employee's back. We might consider an additional break during the day if it doesn't create a hardship. We might consider a spongy floor mat to ease the pressure on joints. All of these accommodations would be considered reasonable by most standards. If we can reasonably accommodate the employee and he can now move 100 televisions across his work station, everyone is happy, but….. what if you haven't identified 100 televisions as an essential duty? Now the conversation gets really difficult. Essential duties are an integral part of any discussion of accommodations and must be included in your job descriptions. What if you have provided these reasonable accommodations and the employee still cannot move 100 televisions across his work station? The ADA does not require employers to "find" a job for the employee with a disability, nor does it require the employer to "bump" someone out of an existing position to make room for the employee with a disability. The long and short of it is, that if ANY employee, including those with disabilities is unable to perform the essential duties of his/her job, the employer has the right to find someone else who can.

As a general rule, there are 4 accommodations that employers do not have to make:

1. Relax attendance expectations. In most business environments, showing up for work is an essential duty of the job, so just because the employee has a disability, doesn't mean that he/she gets to come in late, or leave early or take longer breaks/lunches UNLESS the company has determined that these accommodations are reasonable!

2. Relax productivity expectations. Once the employer establishes essential productivity expectations, the company can hold everyone, including someone with a disability to those same standards.

3. Quality expectations. I can hold everyone, including those with disabilities to the same quality standards to which I hold everyone else.

4. Conduct expectations. I foul language, insubordination, combative behavior, etc. have been classified as unprofessional and unacceptable at work, the company can hold everyone to those same conduct expectations. Even if one of the employees has a mental illness that makes it difficult to maintain control or follow orders.

I don't want to sound cold-hearted with this summary. I have worked with 100's of wonderful people who have had a disability and as a general rule, they are some of the hardest working, most dedicated employees with whom I have worked, but I also understand that the business needs to make a profit and run efficiently. As hard as it may by, the employer may have to replace employees who have disabilities if they are unable to perform the essential duties of their job.

I hope you have found these stories and the thought process to be educational and enlightening. I am still keeping track of the stories and I'm sure there will be a second edition in the not-too-distant future.

Best wishes. Never forget to have the courage to do the right thing and never forget that there are often real people on the other end of our decisions.

Printed in Poland
by Amazon Fulfillment
Poland Sp. z o.o., Wrocław